KICKBALL

DARICE BAILER

The Child's World®
childsworld.com

Published by The Child's World®
1980 Lookout Drive • Mankato, MN 56003-1705
800-599-READ • www.childsworld.com

*Special thanks to Ronnie Polansky for her help
with this book.*

Photo Credits
© AP Photo/The Detroit News/John T. Greilick: 13;
Cheryl Casey/Dreamstime: 20-21; Eric Isaacs/
emiphoto.com: 8-9, 10, 15, 19; Greg Sorber/
Albuquerque Journal/ZUMAPRESS.com/Alamy Stock
Photo: cover; ZUMA Press Inc./Alamy Stock Photo: 5,
6, 16-17 (St. Petersburg Times).

ISBN: 9781503823709
LCCN: 2017944894

Printed in the United States of America
PA02356

ABOUT THE AUTHOR

Darice Bailer has wanted to be a
writer since she was in fifth grade.
Today she is the author of many
books for young readers. She lives
in Kansas with her husband.

TABLE OF CONTENTS

TIME TO PLAY!

Don't sit around indoors. Play kickball outside with your friends! Kickball is like baseball. But players kick a big bouncy ball.

FUN FACT

Kickball has been around for 100 years. It was invented in the United States to help children learn baseball. The game was even called kick baseball at first.

Kickball is fun and good exercise. You can set up a game in a grassy park, at school, or in a large yard.

Ready to play? Grab a ball and let's go!

FUN FACT

Kickball is a popular game around the world. Children enjoy playing in South Korea, Japan, South America, and Canada.

Kickball is set up just like a baseball diamond. The field has a home plate and a **pitching mound**. There are three bases, too.

FUN FACT

Kickball isn't just for kids anymore. Adults have fun playing, too!

THE GAME

The pitcher rolls the ball toward the kicker. The kicker kicks the ball and tries to run around the bases. Just like in baseball, players try not to get **tagged** out.

If a player reaches all three bases and then crosses home plate safely, he or she scores a run.

After three outs, the kicking team and **outfield** switch sides. Both teams have a turn to kick in an **inning**.

Kickball is played for five innings. The winner is the team that scores the most runs.

FUN FACT

Kickball teams have 8 to 11 players. But you can still play with a few friends. Make up your own game with a pitcher, catcher, kicker, and outfielder. Kickers make three good kicks. Then everyone changes position.

KICK AND RUN

Try to kick the ball on the ground. That way you won't kick a high fly ball. **Pop ups** are easy to catch. If the ball you kicked is caught, you're out!

FUN FACT

Players must wait till the ball is kicked to run to the next base. Stealing is not allowed. If the ball hasn't been kicked, and a runner is off base, he's out.

FUN FACT

It is against the rules to throw the ball at someone's head.

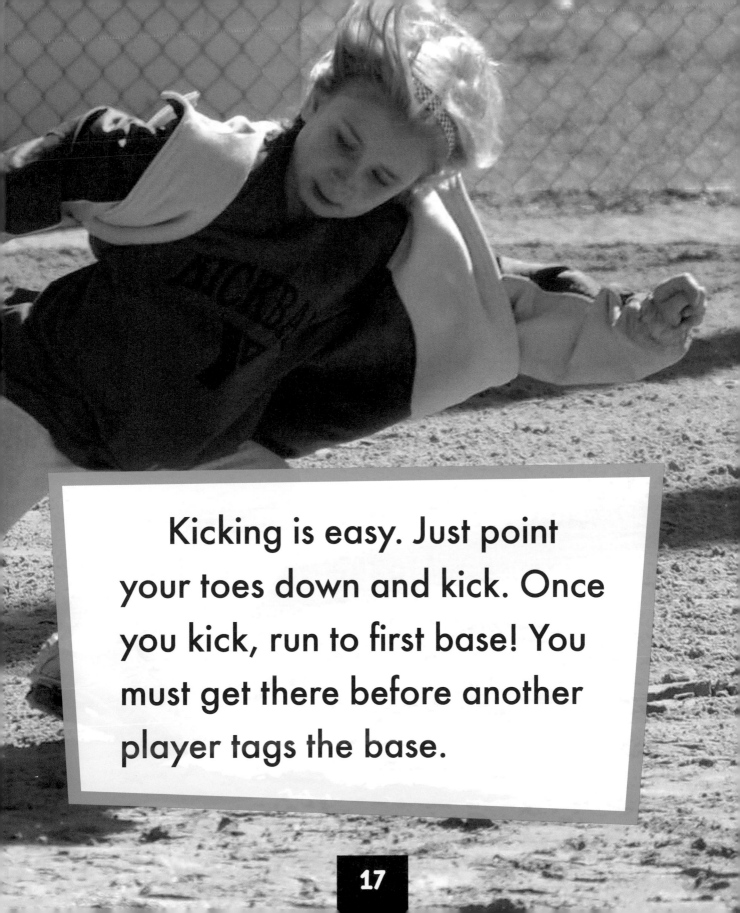

Kicking is easy. Just point your toes down and kick. Once you kick, run to first base! You must get there before another player tags the base.

THE CATCH

Catching a ball that has been kicked means the kicker is out! So always keep your eye on the ball.

But sometimes a ball can't be caught. When that happens, you must get to the ball quickly. Then throw it toward the base where the runner is headed.

FUN FACT

Some people use a soccer ball if they can't find a bouncy kickball to play with.

FUN FACT

In kickball, players must respect each other. They should be good sports. No fighting is allowed!

20

GOOD GAME

Have fun playing kickball. And cheer for everyone on both teams. Kickball is great exercise and keeps you fit. Play a game today!

GLOSSARY

inning (IN-ing): An inning is part of a kickball game. Each team has a chance to kick and play in the outfield during an inning. But if the home team is ahead in the final inning, the game is over and that team wins.

outfield (OWT-feeld): The area of a kickball field that is beyond the three bases and home plate but between the foul lines.

pitching mound (PICH-ing MOWND): The spot on field where the pitcher stands when he begins to pitch or roll the ball to the kicker.

popular (POP-yuh-lur): Something that is enjoyed or liked by many people.

pop ups (POP UPS): A pop up is a ball that is kicked high in the air for a short distance.

stealing (STEEL-ing): Running to the next base while the ball is being pitched or before it has been kicked.

tagged (TAGGED): To get a runner out by touching the runner with the ball.

TO LEARN MORE

In the Library

Dadey, Debbie. *Dracula Doesn't Play Kickball*. New York, NY: Scholastic, 2004.

Stewart, Kenneth. *The Kickball Kid*. Frederick, MD: PublishAmerica, 2012.

On the Web

Visit our Web page for lots of links about kickball:

childsworld.com/links

Note to parents, teachers, and librarians: We routinely verify our Web links to make sure they are safe, active sites—so encourage your readers to check them out!

INDEX